MW00437004

WILLIAM FULLER

Day

Flood Editions
Chicago

break

ISBN 978-1-7332734-1-1

Versions of several of these poems have appeared
in *Adjacent Pineapple*, *Chicago Review*, *Cumulus*,
Datableed, *Erotoplasty*, *Harvard Advocate*, *Hi Zero*,
MOTE, *Oversound Poetry*, *Poetry*, *SPAM*, *The Zahir Review*,
and *Zarf*. "Magic Comma Natural" was published
by Richard Parker's Crater Press. "Arsenic Decision
Pending" was published by Ollie Tong's glyph press.

Design and composition by Crisis
Printed on acid-free, recycled paper
in the United States of America

for Elizabeth

3

Acts of counting arise and pass away and cannot be meaningfully mentioned in the same breath as numbers.

—Edmund Husserl, *Logical Investigations*

LA FRECUENCIA

Schopenhauer writes that "non-appearance of satisfaction is suffering."
Restraint gives rise to discipline. Laughter ebbs in empty cries. The city
of the Gandhabbas is white and powdery—but you can have a horse
carry you anywhere you want. Fold up your thoughts in a clean cloth,
place the cloth on a mirror, then speak these words through a hole in
the sun.

1

TRACTATE

When the great doors of the sky have shot open, and the wind blows all night long for months and days, and billions of insects land on street corners and crawl into bottom drawers, and the distinctions we have painstakingly drawn gaze up at us in anguish, stung by things drilling through them, their nervous chimes cutting through alleys like ropes to drag them away, and in the brief silence before dawn a figure approaches in happy forgetfulness, examining the draft report, glad to have read so thorough an analysis yet suggesting further areas to explore when the time comes to push back against the speaker stuck in his room having spasms, and the violent winter makes an about-face in answer to circuitous forays of messengers met in fellowship to divide the land into higher and lower, but all of a piece throughout, and awakening to a disinterred state, where objectivity manages to betray real feelings before the chimes return to offer the ghost scope to walk in, to bend over the fire and know that nothing except what isn't there is staring back, or to join in a kind of standoff over the whole length of vibration leaking from its mouth, as a scab forms on the rim of the sun—how speechless then: go grab whatever you have access to, bring more of it than you can use, and if no one's coming just now, you can see what's going on, a tremendous sheen is ready to spread itself over the terrifying visions—or stay here and clap quietly while I make some sandwiches, so that if the transcendent phase of the soul fades in and out, and passing pleasures seem more ominous than before, in the orality of inner life, there's still something to snap back from, a place to kneel down in while the injured are carted off, because our strange pallor and inability to speak won't matter when it comes to stoking the future, or driving it to wherever it wants to go, unless the crazy odes start drinking again, thumping the ground with lizard-headed feet, laughing at every strange deduction, and smelling their own hair all night long as a point of aesthetic pride, pure and simple, jarred out of their stupidity.

THE LEASE

No one alive knows what my body is feeling right now but
there's a way of working it out, and there's someone who
knows how to do that, except first we need to wait for the right
conditions, and in the meantime send our strength out into
the disabling humidity to sweat itself into as many drops as re-
quired for oversight of the metropolis called nowhere. (When
I say *my* body I refer to the one I had been renting for many
years until recently.) In the past everything was divisible by
two. People would wait behind a wooden fence while a river of
grass swept by. It was either noon or midnight, and most ob-
jects tended to be either blue or green. The sky was a huge lens
through which the sun and planets and stars were magnified.
Stone towers would perpetually deteriorate, and streets would
trail off aimlessly to the south and east, into the sea. My con-
cern back then was the amount of paperwork needed to doc-
ument all this. Each day I would create a small chart where I
would insert certain private symbols whose meanings I would
guess at. The sun would tilt on its head, trains would travel
backwards, and I'd return home to my perch on the hillside.
Sitting up there, I often saw ships laden with pine cones and

red leaves to be applied to skulls of thinkers in the grass, and these visions lent elasticity to my temperament, allowing me to handle new events by calmly outfoxing them. Complications followed. Despite my training, these became my immediate feelings: aggravation, annoyance, discomfort, disgrace, a sense of oppression, destroyed happiness, inconvenience, indignation, insult, mortification, outrage, vexation, wounded pride, mental anguish, humiliation &c. Yet as of today my eyes have learned to avoid what they look for, and so I follow their lead, focusing on an absent center, so to speak, taking that center to be the thing that one day will envelop me. Most of what remains gazes up at the hazy patch atop the night sky, until certain spells leak down like assistants sent to make a task more difficult, dodging spikes of light. Is *this* what I came here to see, this thing that once lay beneath my feet, its soil exchanged for what I'd occupy, instinctively, through a drone of disappointment? Imagine that I'm speaking of the pain I'm feeling in such a way that you feel it too; and yet I don't feel anything.[1] I'd love to be part of what you're part of, to enjoy some shady dream as it sighs in your ear. And yet.

---

1. See clause VI of the lease.

Is *what* necessary? I take a short trip through time to find someone whose wings have grown sheer or at least impressively faint. I listen to dead voices argue beyond what I can make out, the sentences rolling to no other purpose than to coax remote things into view, even though these fail to maintain interest, and serve simply to punctuate the long night. Yes, amazing. For here on earth seasons grow tired from speech. And there's no recompense without injury. Nobody knows where they stand.

JAMBLIQUE

For the sake of illustration I fall asleep and things change as I breathe them in, the walls becoming floors, the floors becoming streets, the streets becoming fields, while various animals, startled, cautious, move warily up the hill and into the woods, where they revert to a prior state. There are sometimes moments of calm arising in an imagination without the discipline to embrace them. The animals all sense this. They stalk one another through the trees in order to demonstrate their most characteristic instincts. But these become detached from the bodies that house them, which huddle along the circumference, or glide back and forth through small gaps in how they were made. Sounds fall to echoes, roughing out a zone where what one hears matches what one doesn't hear, and adjusts to its shadow.

PSYCHOLOGISM

the milk of paradise
is a subsidiary concept
likely to be removed

a faintly curved
caravan
lights the dark
it has no momentum

a horse
on one string

sobers us again

RULE AGAINST INFINITIES

I never thought in terms of what they would mean to someone else. It was enough to impart color to days. Certain moments reached out to me, which awakened my interest in not paying attention. One could almost distinguish their features as they slid over the grass, combing out thoughts. The sky folded back the essence of its thingness.

Offhand comments do not evidence systematic approximation to what is. Sounds disappear to emerge months later in a waking dream similar to an abandoned course of action. Nothing is simple because one can always transfer responsibility without prior notice (a known issue). Discernment feeds the eye with its clear tongue, washing the blue spheres. Who are last to know are first to be found, their forms slowly removing themselves from visibility, or intermingling with the prospects they have prepared, at some distance, for oblivion. They walk barefoot over sharp stones with pain hurrying them on to tender paths.

Points stretch into lines and lines spread into planes that serve no material purpose.

Soft thoughts make for hard echoes falling into afternoons co-existing with other forms—basic, commercial, institutional. Older days move at different speeds—enough to shake tenuous identifications, although under the same roof absurd pieces endure, however fanciful. The only appropriate distinction is between certainty and uncertainty, and only when the second half doesn't follow from the first. Where are we then, if at all? Somewhere in the south, in the sunshine, late summer, as a distant orb divests itself of familiarity.

Outsiders will soon postulate an interest in physical space and propose a method for assigning that interest. Death would be irrelevant save as an additional problem to solve.

The complex changes sought by dreams are summarized below. Suffice it to say, we gather each morning at the doors of the now and fan out for analysis. One of the steps involves blocking out the sound of voices, which creep up from below to render silence meaningless. For the whole of silence is devotion. And devotion makes silence form. Solid and mysterious, what we see and touch refers to what eludes us, but the reference isn't taken, and in the desert of its absence we uphold it.

Riding in delirium, imagined, remembered, expected, and in conformity with the rule of convenience, the Moon is received by Jupiter in Pisces.

There were other brilliant moments, although it is worth emphasizing how long it took to locate them. It was ridiculous. We sat around for hours putting numbers in boxes, and then in 1911 the Supply Company was founded. I will communicate more detailed information as time permits. But of things in general I remember not having to think very hard. At twilight all the meadows would rise between dreams.

As to the dreams themselves, did they have a sense of their own reverberations? The road leading back from anywhere would suggest so. Tomorrow the flow will seek its limit, fifty years ago. I wish I could explain.

Flaming trees light up the baseboards. Everyone vanishes at once as it were, leaving outlines on the walls. Our instinct is to repeat, without duration, succession. Looking east, we see shapes that used to be there, but they've been modified, *the effect of which we assess by comparison with their state immediately before modification.* They pool in loops.

I was reading to flies in a windowless room. I remember repeating the word *hydrangeas*. Being objective, things relate to other things in their capacity as things. I wish I could explain.

The old square gives itself up to disorder in various flavors, one of which arches into sight from High Street to draw inferences from passersby. Lily is mentioned again. Above long tables below tall windows impulses blend with streaming sunlight and kitchen sounds. What takes place is about to be forgotten in terms of its magnitude.

Having reviewed all this, we invent things to be transformed, ordinary or extraordinary things and the contexts in which they appear, making them large or small, always alert for stray factors, however dimly these impose themselves or find themselves imposed.

This is the billowing larder for years. I put the future at four. The drummer on the bridge puts it between two and three. The others remain where they are, in thick liquor covering properties not observed but brushing against them to create a feeling of proximity, too many to count for now, but something to be conscious of.

The rooms are painted gray and elevate themselves as one enters them. They register the weather with unerring faithfulness. They echo with compound phenomena and sudden fluctuations of visual form.

Influenced by the universal and eternal mind, each breathes in its own unique way, having secured what had been denied by the fact that arms and legs have to take up space.

Time clings to these entities (but does not make contact).

This would almost seem natural had everything lined up perfectly, by which is meant in no particular order except the one that operates inside itself, filling out the frame with small corrections, as whenever someone leaves or goes forth there is an opportunity to take stock and advance one's position in the imaginary space above and the floating field below.

In this climate of despair and doubt bones are ill-fitting, like shoes on a centaur. The ideal starts to flake away, as each day we circle it from a different starting point, making wider and wider rings. That no clear plan had been thought of is obvious. Which sometimes gives us a foothold.

LOBE ISSUES

What is distinctive becomes clearer through hindsight, assuming one can identify today potential sources of return from twenty years ago, and then imagine remaining committed to them over the many line breaks of time. Is faith in knowledge after the fact consolation for an idea that fails? In looking back something new arises that in retrospect feels inevitable, although at the time it was unknown and unaccounted for, something whose immateriality (relative to, say, a dog or a chair) has long since followed its own secret course, and whose nature could not be divined until now, when it quietly extends itself to you, although you are preoccupied with more pressing things, things whose real interest for you lies, oddly enough, in what they carry within themselves of *it*, it alone, spiky but diffuse, damp but tending to dry, brown with rust but still transparent, everywhere, nowhere, or rather underneath those terms, like a substratum, a kind of sleep. If only one could grasp what it is that's essential about it, as it blinks on and off along the margin.

This morning I caught a single thought, coaxed from the end of a pencil, only to watch it dissolve for lack of discipline;

it was a pure play on the shifting space between then and now, a space uncorrelated with the traffic bending slowly down the exit ramp, and the massive clouds approaching from the west. Should there be a correlation? Today is after all the first day of a new month. It tastes of iodine and melts the throat.

THE WATERFALL

A cryptic waterfall lands on earth
between jet trails warming the sea
but the serious ego doesn't move
without answering a question
whose condition it is
never to be asked

and I know, and I know
it flows straight through me
allocating intent as it goes
and the streams are real
soaking incredible gardens
or washing away loose instruments

on the fourth day of the fifth month
of transparent liquid Buddhahood

for Anna

GARISENDA

The town with silver people exhales into the heat, as the least imperfect circumstance drops from a tower that floats against the sun. Clear shapes pass from solitary to solitary, under the long porticoes, or face to face across a ragù. The empty piazza throws burnt colors off stone walls, glowing in mismatched eyes. Is there an angle equal to these falling days? Inside the tower a new formula is being tested and someone strange is moving sideways down the street, with bent fingers jabbing out, circling a cobblestone and stepping back, head twisting around to look at me, leaning forward into the path of what lies ahead, over ground that won't straighten up. Pillars bend the heavy air into clouds. A length of string is used to thread them.

BELLS

As if the color of that tree happened to reflect the water beneath the clouds forming a procession of memories herded into groups from below to meet the last two phases tilting as the sky adjusted them.

Not being there was not the same as standing next to people who were there and echoing what they said with complexities multiplied as soon as they broke free of what transfixed them like the drive toward some invisible but compensatory terminus drained of all surface interest or rather separated from it to allow for deeper investigation of its absence which serves up numerous components that change with each minute movement of the great sleeping particles spread out and linked together over the vast material sphere.

Many have abruptly left the earth or otherwise withdrawn their presence from where we had hoped to encounter them but *do not follow* when the wind springs off tall towers twisting up and down dark streets in search of sun.

Someone opens a door and carries out what feels like an intention to have a shape that persists long enough to be seen for what it is with bell-like clarity but then to fade into the horizon when we rub our eyes in late winter bending south into plays of form and color mixed with a few tears to close out this majestic season of distrust.

Between the glitter of adjacent dimensions and the fullness of last things we grow mad for the future that Ayler found and transmitted through a spirit revived in boxes of thought to resolve what came before into what came after.

2

AT THE HOUSE OF THE RHYMING WEIR

An idea sometimes sweetens by refusing to be expressed, if it attends, solicitously, to this failure, and urges us on to discover the true impediment to its adaptation. In that spirit, and bearing that intention within us, we note here, as elsewhere, there are generally three alternative courses. The *first* is simply to accept without question an explanation someone in our proximity, and whom we know, proffers and then elects to modify out of concern that small details are escaping to set up camp opposite what is being said. The *second* is to surrender one's reluctance to withdraw from the presence of an unsolved problem by grabbing crudely at vacant affirmations that nothing further need be done, that everything to be accomplished was accomplished well before current advocates approached the threshold, coaxed forward by the desire to indulge their own vanity. The *third* is to remain absolutely uncommitted to any specific course, and to insist that the process begin anew each time, contending that no information will ever be adequate to the task of judgment, that the requirements, as they evolve, will make each element moot, or at a minimum place the likelihood of resolution in ever greater doubt over time, with the paradoxical effect that the impulse to continue is not thereby diminished, only channeled into a narrower, more determined form. Although no benefits are likely to accrue from this last course, it's unquestionably the one most often followed, owing perhaps to people's need to test the strength of a membrane designed to repel assault, or their perennial enchantment with kaleidoscopic complications spreading over the earth, as time walks through the sky.

MAGIC COMMA NATURAL

Kind old surfaces bask in wet leaves or lay
themselves down when it's too late to protest
or spend time working up to the time
that time will come without fulfillment or
guarantee that it will come like quick death
flashing footprints in one's electric garden
nearly thirty percent of which has been
allocated to strips of clear plastic walking
across the street to the next generation of lazy
pine trees inwoven with authentic *a priori*
maps of glaciers curling back to the sun,
and if we neglect to mention them before
reaching agreement about the palace of
immortal rest, still quite speculative but wisely
taken offline before the mist comes and
headlights curse right on for the darkness
now out of print although made perfectly
clear there's nothing here except a more subtle
form of absence rising from the ground to
isolate and loosen identity with a blindfold

like a flag and the whole time I'm asleep I'm
actually awake which is analytically true
and little by little standing for something
that's not taking shape from soul vestiges
of plucked silence, then it is all because
of doctrine. But how come no one seems
to know? Sales to related parties sniff
the long corridor leading down to water
before they split apart to let in light or the
feeling of light if not light itself waiting
meekly outside while brains gather in proper
sequence—how come no one asks what to do
next, after the mood thaws but the heart
is still frozen and sinks back into its chair,
indifference being the end of spent energy,
and on a sliding scale of shadows in the sun
looping south with likenesses running parallel,
roots stretch through the air to absorb each
moment as it fails to persist, still alive in
pretense if only briefly? Sentiment indulges
a sudden lurch divided in two parts one internal
and one external that vary in proportion to
distance to the outside from a relatively

young age, feet hanging in the air and known
by three names that tumble down the slow
circle of months to a gnomon standing
in the center, clever but unnatural, whose
bloated fifth interlineated fragment describes
how the shore could slip into cobalt fire.
But is the lake actually rising? Many aeons
have inexquisitely passed in the shape of one
lapidary day brought to bear on amulets
whose power can bridge unimaginable
spaces simply by sitting in escrow, separate
from conventional teachings. Red stars chime
inside white ones and up top Ravenswood
fences roam the ghosts of Bohemia secreting
books inside giant aquamarine letters, with no
guidance from Jupiter and Saturn, blurred dots
in a cold bath of stability that ebbs and flows.
After looking at this from the point of view of
those gone forth to enter harmoniously into
a whole seen only in profile we complete
the section below. The jewels of the heavenly
ear are composite, hard and soft. Longing
for happiness is concluded. Definitions don't

change although affected by lateral motion,
rolling on crystal wheels. Last night we knew
them, had known them, had slept where they had
slept, had wandered off after them, had noticed
things we felt certain they had noticed—storm
clouds smoking up above as major distinctions
spread out at eye level, attaining a diamond-
sharp consciousness in one pure act of dancing
on the tips of leaves unlikely to condense into
anything useful.

I'm trying

to find you

A remarkable sentence is laid to rest, no point in
not ending this way on the downward slope just
outside the city with an attractive spire hooked
to a gorgeous cloud. The reasoning principle lies
buried in the margin of the dominant class or
has been buffeted like a great slow-moving bird.
But that aside the work is still being done, if

to no other purpose than to make that claim,
which walks with a slight limp, the motion not
so much awkward as deliberate, thoughtful,
but then overly hesitant until suddenly
the whole thing collapses into wild variations
on the number three. Who are the others,
edging their voices into the ear of the spectacle,
a whole gallon of which is being wasted on
them, coughing up pins? They hide their
features in clay jars lodged between bodies
stretching lengthwise over remnants of bread a-
sailing on the sea. Removed from time, their
chants now tend toward the forgettable, while
down broad streets and narrow lanes, their souls
are sent back to the place that bore them
with vague but comforting ideas, to wait for
better weather. As a ghost has affirmed,
truth does not contradict the truth. And if
everything flows down to some empty spot,
who benefits beside those holding shares in
that emptiness? Bright sunshine lathers the
stones stuck to the ground. The wind sweeps

through on its way east, full of new contents,
which are unseen but imply a debt secured by
joy, sadness, and desire, or what would exist in
their absence at the next stage, the stage of
impenetrable secrecy, whose faint outlines
match the exact shape of the thing you've lost.

POSSIBLE FACTS

I never affirm, that's not my role. But if there *is* a role it begins where the window meets what presses against it, at the boundary someone who's not here occupies, or rather establishes by virtue of remote influence, or inference I suppose, keeping up the art of thinking it through before putting on a coat and heading outdoors, where all that happens could easily have been predicted given surplus time, although not here, not now, the day poised like a rabbit ready to spring away, or more probably like a dog dozing on a couch, defending the thesis that no thesis has been asserted, so there is nothing to defend, thus avoiding contradiction at the cost of emptying everything into a magic frame through which one might picture what words could express were they abruptly uprooted and sent off to a small room in some foreign city to be accessed only by trained personnel. The city is remarkable for the unpredictability of its weather. What bearing this will have is impatient to make itself known, even to court incoherence, under a faint lamp late at night. Darkness melts into a greater darkness where a few concepts stand out, infecting the room with the intensity of their presence, strangely enough perceived as an aroma, hints of lemon peel, smoke, and cedar. By daylight they rise up starkly disclosed in all their inadmissibility, subject to additional criticism for obscuring more subtle phases of thought through their daily persistence, including weekends. Who moves along this narrow path like a child's voice? Who stares into the sun as the moon crosses in front and the animal kingdom lets out a sigh, as if to say x? Hours later it starts to rain, stranding everyone. I don't remember how I got here, nor which possibilities I may have laid in store for myself back home, or who may have obtained rights to them in the meantime, although why should I worry about this at all, given that no one would necessarily see them as I do, and might in fact regard them as burdens rather than possibilities, which truth be told they are, were I to view them as formerly I might have, in dreams. So I describe a circle extending from east to west, encompassing hills, valleys, plains, accidents, and shadows. I set the circle in motion, then walk back to town. As clear as the sky is, that's how strange it seems to see your face lighting up all the windows. Let me explain—but only after you gather together everyone you want to convince of the beauty of your idea, and then project yourself into a future where your persuasion has been successful. And if that future isn't yet valid, no doubt by the time you arrive there something even brighter and more dramatic will have drawn your focus, perhaps a realm of real stability—as opposed to *here* where ordinary objects plot against you, and time ceases to extend itself to you, that is, duration and succession chase each other out of the room leaving you alone and unaccounted for, consoling yourself with reveries constructed from handwriting, type, print, telex, facsimile transmission, lithography, photography, and other modes of representing or reproducing words in lasting and visible form.

WORLD OF LIGHT

umbrella
testimonies
strong for death
search them
by fingernail
unable to speak
of meadows
below the sea
rare fruits awry
with fire
in transition
to reflection
something new
in view

for Miles, after Tom

CHAPTER TWO

The purpose of this chapter is to familiarize us with key terms and how they apply. Through them we come to know the thing, what's held inside the thing, and who benefits from their combination. This knowledge is so unlike the knowledge of stalks in winter, their elegiac whimpering, or of earth rising up to your shoe-tops—which correlates with consternation and grievous, though temporary, affliction—that we shut our books and stare at it. Whenever such terms fight for space, we should listen to what they have to say; often their uses are far from clear, but without them how could we conceive of what we lack? If they mystify at first, we slowly come to learn that there's something precious they pursue, over the mountain-tops of thought, still warm from the secret of its birth. And with great conceptual industry we begin to rethink our former views, convincing ourselves that if the means by which we achieve what we desire are flawed or false, the sights they evoke might still be real enough, and could be perfect, the foretaste of a state that flutters through all prior states, bringing them to a close.

MAY I?

What is ideality?
Rain pouring over
small pine trees in gradation
all of them turning left toward a place to store them in
and everything else crowding on board
where unsmiling contacts are made then
suspended with an extra syllable
under the mountains of windows
and vertical stripes left by higher powers
to mark where they stood
not so much apart as within *an apartness*
itself contained by a larger quarterly process
fulfilling an annual one, and so on,
night followed by day followed by night.

BASIC PROBLEMS IN POETRY

Something had gotten underway and was proceeding under its own power down the wet street above the town where thousands would never live. I would never live there too, but my perceptions were bent from the start. I could never distinguish between non-identical worlds, nor did I understand how to dilute my own thoughts enough to make them drinkable. Things I read suggested this could be done by developing the proper attitude toward what might in theory transpire given sufficient passage of time. But I don't know what that is. Things continue on in endless space, my good old captain said to me. Meanwhile *session one* began by revoking the law against breaking promises. Egregious examples were set out on a plain oak table overlaid with butcher paper. Crayons were handed round and then deposited into a cylinder that appeared at the window. The session turned strange when one of the examples lurched through the room, calling the others names. My right eye became distracted at the very instant I knew that this may not really be the case. So be it, lights flickered in the sky and tall white letters shone brightly, as we easily saw for ourselves. Out of them the future could be read, and the things that would exist in it could be seen hiding amid the clouds. There was nobility in these prospects, which varied depending on the character of the grain being roasted. Now was not the time that then was, but then no time was. And although heavenly trumpets tendered cakes of phrase, I knew Satan's Kingdom had a hand in this. Therefore *session two* called for a different approach. I drew up a map that showed us here, where the black dots are, with our destination being there, at the edge of the fir trees. I traced a fibrous line between them and off we went. Maybe it was too soon after his death for things to have stabilized, because when asked about staff reductions all eyes turned gray. As we floated along, a sense of futility followed us at a respectful distance, occasionally stopping to rest or take notes. The dark air grew thick, and our progress was stalled thanks to *Preternatural Stupendious Prodigious assistance by the Devil given thereunto*. A low theater crept up from the east. I presupposed its existence before analyzing it. Many times I'd done the opposite and found myself carefully arranging shadows while the objects that had cast them wandered off, pursuing whatever desires or whims arose in them. In fact this became something of a trend over the years, until I counted myself among those movable shadows, whose relative independence only affirmed their contingent, gratuitous character. So I assessed the current situation according to what depth of conviction I could muster about the judgments to be made. For example, was it sunrise or the middle of the night? We were wide awake, certainly. And there were birds singing. But a sheet lay over the whole village. Did it appear then, as it does now, that the same question could receive thousands of different answers, and that we may as well have been consigned to the nether side of some unknown planet as to have been where we were? This didn't seem likely, or rather there was no need to exaggerate the case or its effects, even as the west wind swept through each tentative disposition. What felt clear was the sense of a mental journey cut short by open-mouthed disbelief turned despairingly toward an empty corner of the room that had suddenly enclosed us, as the dim light from a sconce revealed a single, round object approximately five feet away, either on the floor or hovering just above. I called out to it; it called out to me. Next door someone said, "Wait for the Face Man to come." Whether I knew to whom this referred I can't say. How could such a problem be borne without the elusive gauge of poetry? Was there any way the situation could have offered me a more refined sense for what was lacking, as I struggled to humor it into giving a hint what the next step should be? But there was no next step. Present and future were simply abandoned to the insensate devouring gorge. Alternatively, the round object could have been a kind of poem, like Wyatt's "In Æternum," although I'm adding that just now. At the time I had no idea what it was or whether it mattered for me to know, or even whether its status as an object was worth confirming. I did nevertheless try to confirm it. I understood x to be true owing to reasons a, b, c, and d. In reality, though, x was false, for those exact same reasons. The next day I stood waiting for a train. By then someone else was living inside me, which changed the problem completely.

RETENTION

While the individual sentences are autonomous and self-contained, they are also linked by shared internal elements too small to see. The second sentence opens on to a garden with two green chairs. The third sentence darts away like a rabbit. In the fourth the golden tortoise of misconception doesn't absorb any point being made or not being made.

There is no fifth sentence.

MURMURING GENERATION

This day is like a new arrival recognized from before as what abides here and never leaves but plants itself in one place, talks about everything being talked about with an intensity clutched up inside at arm's length along a perimeter where attention fails to focus on any one thing as it takes flight into a morning of steam and staggering footsteps moving slowly to the east, then brushes by itself going the opposite way, unconcerned by the flesh of fact, whose influence turns out to be more prominent than we had thought, if only for right now, while we wait for someone to show up and tell us how both halves of the house are doing. Or will we be told we're doing it all wrong by concentrating on the task and the steps it takes to complete it and not on the penumbra of feelings that has descended on us like a weird mist, launching itself into our eyes in such a way that we can't observe it, or if we could we would mistake it for a quiet room full of empty space where certain attitudes are present that might defuse all this negativity and give proper acknowledgment to those deserving it, with gestures that don't always go awry or stand there looking in the wrong direction when the wave hits. What is it, beautifully, that you see? Rivers washing the sky.

SUCCESSION PLAN

furry metronome
obtains human birth
so hard to stop
purblind dirges
rain tortures
esemplastic
farcical acts
to follow
the power of one
warehouse spittle
fails to entertain
the gorgon
once fermentation begins
Tukutukupakata
the mountain sacred
to output traits
of quick-drying
misfits
leans over
the visual world
like some

misgoverned

beef stew

conglomerate spinoff

flipping open

random bins

and telling us

how coffee tastes in the

upper branches

stricter Botanology

sketches out

a sky

ready to

plummet

thus ends

chapter two

it is not

identity

unraveled or

a vacant house

far inside

a mirror

that went unpled

all urgency fled

cantankerous

formalization

recalls

something like a duty

can't explain

think it's

vibrating

infrastructure

or shares of

tuna salad

ready to

cut in line

at discount

whammy bar

we wan

go see

new light

on old trains

frosting imps

code blue

rake silence

into rows

rumors

diversify themselves

bouncing along

one in each hand

stamped or metered

whether true

or not quite true

biofuel pilot

has begun

while Thursday's

frack numb

portraiture

or mi-solo

alt smacks

both ways

or fluke

into small bites

at rest

cheeky

supposititious

fingernail

swoops

to clean

bacon grease—

the fickle and the faint

through the contents

of their pockets

poke

gusting lily folk

de Chicago

don't mistake

the crate of anger

for the throne of judgment

trees fall into

crescent moon

Venus plucks

a semiquaver

like cheese

on a spoon—

emphatical

Babylonians

jump and prance

to the new

compensation

structure

vertically sliced

ivory gate

hardly this but nearly
that
the foamy
prophets
launch themselves
into strategic thought
one of them is clearly
"obtuse-sagacious"
to quote Kierkegaard
meaning what
remedy remains
"when time shall be
no more"
but to soar
into the sun
whose arms
stretch out in space
diffusing
possibility

TROPOSPHERE

Being committed to life inside this particular dream felt like a betrayal of that other dream which had advantages in how it dealt with the problem of an external stimulus. A thoughtful compromise has made things simpler if less uniform. There's a haze of incredibly detailed stuff that's never been seen before. And look at the people, reaching into the pockets of time. Their eyes flash dim in all directions of *and or* and *if* to spread their last warmth. Brightness slow to upward flight marks the full blossoming core. A remnant grows into a theme or draft of more intense feeling. Put it aside.

All the brush has been cleared as an example of what can happen when things look back toward the principle—this I know and know full well, that no heart opens without schemes emerging. Reach for them as they fade across lives laid end to end through a needle's eye. Part gift, part obligation, part paraphrase (books, brochures, bulletins), part nullity. Small wires connect *peculiar syntheses that have a continual or discrete coinciding of sense.* A penknife pricks them. Looking straight through what's here to what shades off until any ordinary person could grasp it, would I grasp that much less? Put it aside.

Objects wait for us locked in a system that calls for ever more extensive views to vivify the air and the clouds and the sun until nothing resembles what it was before. We've seen how things play out, when boxes come and access is turned off and the coherence that had roughly been achieved begins to melt. Puddles like eyes. To frame the oracular, leaving things as they stand without, *or carry them on by night, fumid cadger, this possible form of yours & what strange hours of divine peace,* find them within. Whose memory are you? The thought that it's not my dream makes its way inside furrows of panic to wake from. There was a shop or a series of shops on a narrow street. The day was cloudy (or was not). A deer crossed the hill in front us, followed by tiny fragments of bone or white blossoms.

The window fogged up as though that were the case. The spaces between the seats pressed against it.

Doing what needs to be done, yet we know there must be more to do, sailing on the verbal sea: have you film upon your eyes hung with what catches fire? Words deal color, shape, fragrance of sweet earth underfoot, gathered succinct. A dark luminosity shakes in the heat. And if that comes and goes there's still the dependable idea of emptiness.

Here too small deserts can form.

Yesterday was the last day in conformity with prior law. A glittering overcast morning, moist music breathing on the façades. On the shoulders of time sat pathos and tedium. We lined up the chairs according to their colors and then sat down to watch. Over the course of the ensuing hours impressions came and went, and some of them were retained in the memory. Of these the most remarkable tended to reinforce one another, causing us to experience them as one sustained event, which slowly rose up above the rough, exposed surfaces. This has now happened twice.

How tightly that smallest planet tracks the sun.

Thinking about variations from day to day seen through windows rendered opaque from a busy network of fine scratches, with waves of sunlight blocked by the names of trees and a certain helplessness pulling at my sleeve. The elastic past rises with no mortal sound. The hands of clouds reach down inside me. Everything else appears stable.

You will succeed in being more than you are by being less of what they need—a shape whose outlines fail to appear. Down by the station walls are crying, speaking, rattling on. Birds arrive from Jupiter. I collect feelings and apply them to phenomena—moiety, dragonfly, Keel Row. A bear on a bicycle rides by. Does routine tasks. Lies down beside the rising water, whose green arms frame a ragged thought between two fantastic streams of light. Ready to be absorbed when spring drifts into fall, based on a system, for *the past does not change*, new growth touches the way things are, slowly built up, these somnolescent footsteps, with homage to every stage, for touch, pressure, warmth, and pain.

Not forgetting the raw place where nothing endures and nothing changes. The sun twists punctually. No chance to make the train.

BAGATELLE

a capacity to exist
and to linger

like a straw hat
inching up a hill

take the case of the person
after it was produced

the notes are thinking
that's not the tune

suddenly the trees
are disappointed

for they have been
tampered with

in abstracto
by the sky

PLANETS AND SUNS

I am
languishing
figures in a wood
obstinate or deep blue
a luxurious empire
I'd not seen before
of disguised hypothetical statements

and you are sitting
at the western vanishing point
half-whistling bright colors
when the train comes along
inside a vibration
without birth
without death

THE CONJECTURE

In your place I propose a tower of snow or crisscrossing ruts viewed vertically with no apex or uniform approach to join their opposed principles. The correct thing to apply in each case avoids being seen, and the map remains obscure despite the clarifying imposition of conventions. Not metaphors for agency, these elastic spawn were soaked in vinegar prior to the nineteenth century, well before the rule of law came to an end, and parties could seek relief simply by running their mouths backward. There was nothing then but landlocked time looking up at the sky from this exact spot. Whereas now basis bends with the storm. A delicate framework might be ripped apart to let in light, but to see what? An arrogant, volitionless agent on whose behalf? Or it turns out these are not clouds, nor does the sky present itself to the viewer with any purpose in mind other than to be taken as objective. It floats along the valves of the storm to the nebulous antipodes of an argument, the wrong place willingly substituted, or made less significant for having been wound on a spool of words. Meanwhile she said the light was green, and though it was true that she said it, what she said wasn't true. The whole idea is to whisper yourself into activity and make no exception for your state of mind. For light once was dark, and nothing was sustained by it, no pulse, no gesture, no performance relative to peers, only huge depths tasting of ashes with a smooth finish suggesting landscapes devoid of any compelling features, pinpoints divested of pins. There doors were windows, windows were doors, time was reversible, and people remained seated to achieve the goals of inanimate things, while inanimate things made music despite their silence, and what could be borne at what cost sought companionship in underwriting that cost, on the twenty-third floor of the Twenty-third Psalm, in a conundrum piled high like dirty snow, with rock-like intensity staring down at the ground or foundation of the ground. This last point should be outlined in phosphor. The dance section begins now, is that your testimony? Which lies are labyrinths? What wandering flesh? Whose gleaming representations through frayed showbread ecstatically are to be gleaned? You picked up a pencil and bit off part of the sky. The sidewalk vanished into the storm. A lamp burned inside the brain to reveal the workings of an intelligence skilled at drawing stray material signs into its passageways. Remote from knowledge, your impressions woke slowly to cancelled ambrosia, and in ten minutes your arms were numb, and the tent you slept in destroyed by the wind. Is it even relevant that you were ostracized? One more day of this perhaps, one or two highly specific remarks, one or two hard feelings, nothing left unsaid, flowers in the snow. In fact the dawn knelt before you every day you continued to exist, correct? The angle of your vision was impaired by no objects. The walls wove themselves into you. But was something dislodged by the storm and so unable to maintain its independence without applying to authorized parties for support? In due course did they take up the application? Clouds sowed rain in the faces of speakers, in the faces of readers, reading the chains of the storm, tracks across a frozen field. From the perimeter you see everyone. No one sees you. Your pulse pounds out an electric appetite for interruption and delay. (The manner of your transcription betokens a regrettable convergence of elements that had sought a different destiny.) For truth is like a snowflake in all but uniqueness, and disquiet will not admit to basic illations, or assert that analysis really is interminable. "It's hard to tell the difference when they take their hats off" is an excuse not quite present to the ear, or born of the chattering landfill of the mighty dharma king, who rescinds himself note by note, passing over the switches that regulate his meaning. May your hands be changed into snakes. Out of respect for automatic voices I now reverse myself. Was that a different you just then, swinging past me? Your first words were like animals— although that impression was modified by their successors, who, by keeping their feet off the railing, so to speak, showed some consideration for those seated below. Next morning six bright spirits rebuilt the courthouse larger than before. After this the sun failed to rise for six days, yet the air still sparkled in its absence. Or did the spirits space themselves at lucid intervals to link together all these reticent, deceptive, and evasive souls? How much uncertainty could there actually be in a person's voice, after the incredible pains taken to put the picture together, methodically coating its entire surface with a lack of ambiguity? But the unconscious monkeys around with the word *reasonable*. We're now in the sixth generation of snow people, and there's no sign that any of them wishes to be a martyr for new modes of being. You shake your hands to shake out the cold or trace the outlines they throw in successive images extracted from a sidelong look. A woman fiercely rotates her arms. Barely awake, a man questions his hawk, his horse, and his dog. She was here after all, let the record show, then fled through the broom. Which of you is neediest, or whose face most calmly shapes fear? The window melts fire in the fading light. Someone you trusted may have been, and in fact was, derelict as to what we've just been talking about. Is that a moose?

Upstairs thoughts put on their clothes. We're not clear whether this may already have happened although everything hinges on sending memory down forking paths while continuity races ahead to prepare for it. Tell me, have you ever seen me? I need you *there* in order to exist. The figure, absorbed in secondary qualities, doesn't know, doesn't answer, pivots in the snow, retreats, covers itself with the veil of the horizon; the modest mind lies still. Think about the map again, how it looked in the mirror, how the destinations lined up though the values were wrong. Later we released its artisanal twin, save for one small flaw that flared along a golden ring and petered out in silence. Whether this was evidence wasn't disputed because unknown. The peaks of sky fold in, inducing a kind of exploratory trance or lassitudinous wandering. In the deep cold the threat to *mash you down like butter against the sun* impresses. Look back into the past and see what else you can distinguish. This is the final demonstrative—it writes itself on the wing of what you know, but you are not what it means when it mentions you, nor are you other than that, fluted indifferently into decaying sound to arrive, or not, where you are or were, present when absent. Was this the standard you applied? When the cold fled those responsible for it soon found other things to do. But memory kept raising up weird shapes. And hypothetical statements laid them down.

THERE

No closer to an ideal, words are noises—
beneath the white dome are chambers
for stacking boundless multitudes of them

arsenic levels built up

3

DAYBREAK

At daybreak one saw receptacles from the day before and in
those receptacles lay strings of associations about to disappear.
Over and over people got up to leave. There was a constant
humming or swinging of doors, then everyone would linger
in the hiss. This happened almost every day and it seemed ab-
surd. It was someone's whole world carried on someone else's
back, and you needed time to get clear of it. There were those
who wore haloes of lights that flicked on and off as they turned
this way and that. They had built floors for large machines
wherever they were. They had built weird towers with heavy
wooden steps climbing up to nothing. Some days clouds would
swallow the sky and the path became lined with polyp-like
jewels shaking from the inside, hundreds. One closed one's
eyes to see them. Inside each there was room to extend yourself
thinly yet broadly in a way that encouraged convalescence but
also put you at odds with everything else. For these were always
damp and limp and inched along over hard ground. But some-
how out of them rose entities to be reckoned with, dark blue
overhead looking down with eyes emanating soft red light sug-
gestive of infinite changeability, turning legs and arms into
snakes or other creatures at every street corner. Their cries gave

a shock, compressing life into a few sharp points soon dissolved by others' presumptive horizons. We were all talking about them—were they somewhere above or behind that ridge with the sound of bells in clear air breaking in, too much to contemplate directly or not enough to parse according to our collective experience that was ineffective in determining what they were up to, which they themselves didn't know but acted like they did? Strange these thoughts whether thinking them or watching others do so. Whether the train was looping around the parking lot, or people were wearing yellow hats and so on. Up here all is covered by a thin fabric, nearly transparent, as broad as the moon. And in the waning hours you shut everything out to concentrate on one stray detail, hoping to pull from it some fact on which to base a new spirit built from smoke and mist and cloud, that staggers upright then just starts walking. You stand apart near a bird, like a nuthatch or creeper, barely signaling what's going on in late January. Things get twisted around, eyes shoot up arches while breath bleeds inside so-called purer forms. Once in a while you try to coax out what's been hiding in the woods. Cases like this are bound to fascinate, or at least inspire discussion about from whence one's authority flows, the tax consequences, disclosure requirements, the material contents and elements from which they arise. Are these finally the objects themselves, reached by distant ladders, from moment to moment ceasing and coming to be with retrograde movements performed by a single agent behind a single door? You were telling me all of this was given to a sick person to burn. The dignity of that practice was then lifted up and carried to some small unknown region near Greece. There mortification was superseded by begging, and what is called the nectar of human decency was forever set aflame in the normal course of events how beautiful. *One night we held ourselves to the narrowest train of thought as it crossed a dark field, its light bearing down on us.* Start again. If without lifting a finger we could move the entire place and its multiplicity of goods, including sixty-four thousand sounds, into a convenient abyss or chasm, there would be no incentive not to do so if only to stimulate one's glands. Slightly north, at the entrance to *Il Ghetto*, components once belonging to sensation had set out on their own to create new blends that they aged in glue pots under a ledge. We paused to watch, astonished to feel everything tensing up inside. Do we live in some elongated spheroid? Maybe an aspect, I don't know, of some entity of which we are a part? One explains that this is who we are, this is what we do, we have no other purpose or goal than this, our lives consist in this, hunched over a shadow held out at arm's length, and remembering a pale sky from long ago in which there was nothing to be gained by looking up into it, into transparent uninterrupted thought as it flies down some corridor where everything is clearly distinguished but nothing can be identified, save for one long black table around which four "deliciously appalling" concepts sit. From here they look like skeletons with loose-fitting bones. Their electric ecstasies slide from brain to brain, along the delicate iron shelves of the helical upward path. Later they ride home in yellow moonlight, on a frozen chain of foaming fire. And behind them sits the perfect order of death in higher dignity of inner evidence. See then how the same thing applies to life. We make a new beginning, only to become aware, by damping of sound, that a partition is being interposed, and that the head once full of light is closing its eyes for the last time.

In the front car people wrap themselves around each other with real aggression, until no one can yank them apart. Knowledge is less secure when days are flung off on the way to somewhere else. And right now something happens I can't quite account for. It leans its head against me, seeking guidance or awaiting word that all this shapelessness can be resolved to a simple quantum, so to start again with a clean approach and clear standards, pushing aside quirks, to mark out an exact point on the skin of each phrase.

LEAVE-TAKING

created objects

are uncontrollable

dilating

the heart

on peacock

paper

so deep and thick

the principle

of all principles

is but a play

snuffe your candle

one more time

victoria eleison

but remain visible

to no one

and against that

consider the where

of what is

or what's based on it

and what in the meantime

may have accrued
while procuring all
that isn't all
at the empty *x*
of huddled roads
head shoulders arms
not of earth—
the sound of them
sounding out
a particular sound
not to decay
as ordinary sound
and not of itself
but bound over
to the next
not to be remembered
successor sound
compared to it somehow
a little shorter
slightly sharper
more intense
but less effective
like great four-footed beasts

of the star soul

whose whimpers

enhance the horizon

until the farm

glistens

and the regional

essence of experience

brings into focus

a finger pointing down

or gesturing at a screen

whose light

washes in and out

enough to sicken

the rest of my life

with sweet piles of memoranda

spread like mustard

over windows tilted up

into a flock of clouds

to reflect

an absolutely perfect

restlessness

which is absurd

not being a thing in space

it splinters
like rain
whose blanched
abstraction
is *not* what you heard
beside a golden
garden wall of fog
and to the right
the divine stream
of human ambiguity
wide awake by default
and for your unripe
reasoning
the conifers and roses
lean back
over the path
to become
one another's
messengers
quietly flowing
through the body's
glade
lessening

tactile properties

upstream

from sensation

at the null point

of mazes

down from the sky

whose backward mirror

returns a backward gaze

through fan-shaped gaps

scattered inside it

clarifying remote non-worlds

with dabs of solvent

to mingle

at dusk

unsaid, unsaid

a pause

to stream away

for you are

raw existence

deprived of oxygen

or a lovely boat

of factual

knowledge

unmoored

split apart

or the shadow

of a quintessence

embodying

a pulse from elsewhere

a sphere called multiplicity

its yellow eye

partitioned

into pure forms

not possible here

undulations

without time

and nothing left

of active states

to twist in the sun

or wind into

dark water

rich and spotless

a scintillant blue sense-field

expanding on all sides

bearing no trace

of what it clings to

in calm

excluded

lodestar

analysis

steadfast or recalcitrant

or slow to be

fulfilled

by clouds

pedaling hard

against thick

foam shadows—

their veins

are silver

and naively present

their plumed embroidery

in propria persona

is not

how they appear

with a hiss

in every word

flicking away

what you are

as I am—

made hollow

by air

and rambling on

about the psychic fields

of this *hermeneutikon*

to bear

the tender motionless

outgrowth

unlit

or languish

in it

sniffing

promissory notes

of what's to come

folded into

the old moon's

elapsed phases

at the pure point

of nowhere

shone through

as though it were true—

things had to be

things this way

like bird music
I once heard
when I was
stationary
beside it
or was
of a piece
with what it became
the green-walled sea
of objectivity
and how did this happen
in a space
no air can navigate
was it the turquoise shed
known as *building three*
that disengaged itself
exactly thirty
years ago
slipping through
the noose of thought
to lay down paths
for alleys
"still waiting

for death"
in modes
and joints
and wings
and spears
who saw
the first phrases
slump down
in soapy water
held fast
by the wrist
of the evening lights
to pause
right hand extended
toward depthless shapes
all three strata
hovering before me
to repeat
at will
the four infinitudes
in steel silence
with hints of
a visitor

crossing the Milky Way

tailgate down

wares displayed

the majestic

umbrage

over visible and invisible

becomes prey

as I would say

to cloud's blood

in midair

long deceased

but remember

what was said

as if you could see it

suspended—

are such feelings adequate

to this quarter's surplus

placing them where

the stream reflects

rose sun glow

on endless fields

staring out

at compressed patterns

of the gleaming day

projected

into mental time

ablaze

with things that have fallen apart

but two percent more efficient

than regular time

not to exist

now

in the customary sense

raising and lowering limbs

sideways through the park

in deference

to a secondary power

subject

to effacement

in whole

or in part

a moment of one

being a shape

of the other—

sleeves

rippling
crazily
away from the face
inside
the round square

ARSENIC DECISION PENDING

Decorated with small animals, the plant of truth, I now know, is full of stars, stored overnight, bracketed, punctual, aloof. In a quiet corner of the room dust builds up self-confidence. We speak of a unifying substance, an object returning home, a triad ruled by a monad, a waterfall to drink from in what language.

Tufts of river drift toward integration. Not in a daze, as some report. Time turns out to be a trick, which I infer from the acts of owls.

Carried to work in a bag kept next to the door, or crouching in the fallen leaves, like a meditation on the angle of sacrifice, It neither begets nor is begotten. The bag is in a strange mood, resolved to trap forever everything contained inside it, save the impulses of what chooses to remain there. Which emotion does this stir? No description can be adequate so none is attempted. A decaying spirit spreads throughout both worlds to supervise routine contingencies.

Neither back nor forth, a pause indifferent to both, a resting place, a pile, a heap, a brain, a flame, a clarity of purpose, a box inside a box, progress to be made when need arises, a piece, a moment, a mistake surrounded by words, its penumbra, a flag in starlight, the set of all these, to regulate wasted time, snow, air, earth, and where they lead.

This slowly becomes true, no part, no whole, no top, no sop.

Of the three windows, the middle is the largest and shares with those on either side certain properties behind which people are being let go. What isn't generally is, its strange energy dangling oh dear.

Within reason to soar in test of boundlessness from this very two-dimensional plane, which goes on and on.

Don't try to change my mind, it is unchanging, although unfinished. It has no shape beyond the shape shaping it, close to the bone of the not yet nor ever yet to be, running fingers through its own isolation, like and unlike, a pattern pulsating in air, proportions mixed in shade, nothing more.

Water glides through the night, ragamuffin style. To the left is a wax tablet containing the riddle of daybreak. The morning star sifts through delicate blue.

This is possible but not obvious.

You tell the story of what transpired within the episode you're thinking of, and though it didn't happen, it left the strong impression that it did. To speak concisely, the principles of one are constrained by the principles of the other. Together they form a matrix for anything worth speculating about, in which details resist incorporation into the larger market, like a box of needles orbiting a silver chair. Outside, people succeed one another so rapidly that it's difficult to view them as distinct. Yet as they slide forward light plays off the reflection of their implied basis in time. They seem to move in pairs.

Since those days we've developed disciplines to sustain us, although occasionally a thought escapes to set up shop just beyond the perimeter, and late at night the attic lights suggest a report will soon be riding around in a wheelbarrow.

Oka Banzola. How many firmaments on the way to work, the north star at the base of the neck, a rock for all scissors, and the receptacle take note of. Different and same define the frame, but I can't work it out—to know, to guess, to believe, attentively, judiciously, to rub my eyes.

Days stomp down. Once they've begun, they last till they're done, then pass into the void. Angels wait for the howl, regret and make a sign. I thought I caught a glimpse.

Which doesn't mean stop and start over again, or head back to some inner chamber for a point of view to take off from, a lodestone in the snow with sensing surfaces—on the other hand, let's talk about what's available, and our level of comfort with something that doesn't quite conform to its own essence—like a person who can't get things done. In the end, the phrase fits, the hammer hits, the fever wakes, the up stays up and bitterness roots—its presence is lustrous. It is either one of two, or two of an unknown number.

What's no longer here remembers what was, and constantly makes room for it, moving through its empty volume, like a shadow through a mirror.

Light and *heavy* change seats for the trip home—upturned faces float. No end in sight except the obvious, the memory of which turns white. No when without where.

Keep talking brief pleasures, the clouds they do grow high.

Weariness and sleep of all things data bring forth too much. How long you give one look the color of sand. Silhouetted air stalk, gulls on ice. See-through figures of each new person entering the room. Vole parity, within a bridge of small cups.

Probable or possible or doubtful meanings catch a whiff on the hill. *Hyperbolized nothing* takes well-reasoned steps. And then it becomes time to reflect on what had gotten us this far, some combination of play-acting and acumen outside a door where one can see inside without entering, and by observing produce thoughts like scrubland flowing out from bodies of all sorts, contracting or dilating based on their different properties, the larger and the smaller behaving in opposite ways, before discharging microtones that melt in dazzling pools of fire. It's hard to imagine where anyone could go from there. But word came down. Gradually it's understood the next stop arrives out of sequence, and the chimes to signal it cut themselves into pieces that refuse to sit up and write but instead offer to get additional resources before falling back to advocate for meaningful movement toward a future that won't spoil their loose plans to lay out wares. Morning again and gray cold jumps the line. The conductor closes in. There's a vague sense of a missed destination, of a storm in the station. Move closer, for she has come to know when to start and when to end and whom to fear and where to be off to.

How to eat what they teach you. How to mix white and red. It's well to be well, to know that *a* and *c* are well, well, their slow awakening to offhand remarks and molded smoke gone somewhere to be near you. The aftermath is threefold, grunt, howl. Consideration comes first but only if spent cash won't do. Release is next with deferred wet signature, in numbness to account. Indemnity goes last, the human grub all grown with swelling in both ears.

A sea-green skull may *not* be influenced by the interest of any third party or by motives other than the accomplishment of its own disintegration. The sun crests over burning switches and police activity east of track three. How to avoid being mistaken for a deer that is gracious and well-behaved but sometimes wanders off. I think there may be some mechanism I've failed to account for, as I look out this morning.

Years later flesh and sinews fail. So much has been omitted that we abstain from noticing. Talk, chat, converse. What were you planning to be encased in? Does it matter that the paths to nowhere are picking up speed through backyards violently split apart by lack of maintenance? I don't mind what these people say so much as the way they say it, their mouths and throats pounding against lungs and the wild skyward leaps of nerves being bored out. With a shrug I become visible again, two at a time, calling out from the crib, through decades of air, *William Byrd*.

I know your face. Honest I do. It's nothing in your favor—the wind puffs up structures more like words than things, although words *are* things, amoeba substitutes, units of attention, tissues under pressure to pass awareness from you to you to you, or nobody to nobody, but only for a minute, in a succession of minutes, old and new minutes, and whether they endure.

Riding in the moonlight with gentle scholars who stack their deeds against the cold. What is the effect on exposed skin? It's not too late to say its proper name. Where no one was, I am, amended and restated. Set the brakes. Release the brakes. Brake test complete.

The body shuffles back and forth until parts don't fit and the voice cuts out and sand builds up where bones won't go. What you feel is exactly what *it* feels, only the descriptions differ.

Here you both are, an unknown number. Bell and cup, bell and cup, city on a lake. Slower and slower days, whither ghostly red sentinel. Those clouds I am on a path to, the current looped in to accommodate, the wall on its side waiting for eyes to construct it. Remember this scene before it evaporates. The smallest piece holds everything in place.

OBJECT

love doesn't die
but pools in darkness
after eyesight fails

or color data appear
in someone else's shape
without disturbing it

WINDOWPANE

Before you put it out you should line it up, they said. The hand-books all said the opposite. No wonder I set everything aside when the time came and worked my way downtown to a leaf-less, dreamless dimension, carrying a stalk with shallow similarity to the proper name not spoken here, Jesus, save on special occasions when letters would come and we'd all scatter like tinctures on tiptoe, communicating a charge to the visual field one closes one's eyes to—birds deep in the air at a range exceeding imagination along a single string knotted and pulled tight to bind time and place against whatever wanders there without undermining the assumptions that caused it, wonderfully, to occur. That old heart of yours burrowed away, lights flashing until the last day of 1971. The quickness had grabbed hold of you then, not letting go until 1982. We spent hours and months buffing quarters outside the station, with the dark pebbles of upper atmosphere melting all the ribbon-candy fences to signify a secret abundance of ungrown fruit for transition from "who are" to "who will be," individually, that is, not me but someone I once was, adjacent to me. No wind could be more luminous weeping there. Lightning drummed the desperate heart of a noun lifting up its heel against the honeycombed one who understood midnight speech only to slink away before the silent preposterous meditation clapped too loudly. Then the door refused to open without everything coming to a complete stop ringed by an emptiness out of which peered the small kangaroo-like face of a fawn. Nothing could unfloat this sapling of perception and its moist insight into what, if anything, could be done with us. Days later, we stumbled onto a formation boasting three noble apertures that bordered a field pledged to animals, and in their debt you stood apart, turned into shiny glass. Through these apertures millions of words were streaming into sentences that broke off in your mouth, dousing your hair with exogenous factors. I placed the leftover molecules in heat-resistant cups, then sat down at the back of the room where the slides were barely visible—one seemed to say "serpent" although it could've been "scimitar" or "section"—a code section?—the Code that regulates amazement like a great dreaming dome echoing with cries of perfunctory things, sandwiches, trashcans, deep but dazzling, or the discreet sound of a shelf of words separating branch from leaf, plus "something else as well," he says mysteriously, lost in the soft center of nowhere, clicked shut inside a flowering eye? So I went downstairs past the sentient adjudicators, whose dark canvas stretched out over a quavering voice straining for air amid new forms of thought. "I kind of let myself go," said the voice, which belonged to a remarkable snail-like organism off to my left. "But it's *their* fault," the creature explained, pointing through the window at the clouds. As I walked away, the clouds began to dance for benefit of an imaginary spectator, who held up an old map of the ecliptic like a hand of bright pins pushing back at the sky. But the moon had fallen asleep and all the secret zones had fled into the fruit trees without making full use of the lies allotted them. A little question hung there dating back to the days of the porcelain deities who strummed away in apparent detachment: *Are individual forms posited and clung to in their multitudinousness only for the sake of putting us on notice of their non-existence?*

Peace at daybreak. Someone was up betimes, some ludicrous bird trying to unravel the groaning light. If, dear animal, you really mean what you say, then we're ready to listen, although we won't lift a finger to confirm this. The sun floated out, giving the sidewalk something to think about beside shuffling pedestrians, whose thoughts lent color to their captivity here, bound by acts of counting and sermons washed ashore from the soaked air of who knows where. That night I dreamt I was walking on a rope bridge over a rising river while dreaming another dream in which I was doing the very same thing. Two umbrageous themes had developed as joint tenants, only to leave in trust.

Then I remember one evening on the terrace, when we sensed things sensing us, so we kept quiet and looked up to the absent moon, in a caricature of inquiry which soon enough became earnest, as the views disclosed for the purpose of valuing that vision vibrated with detail, full of what lay richly at hand in a motionless hour. The difficulty was this, that winding among us were extra forms just below the level of attention, at a threshold complicit in what we think we recall as opposed to what we try to reconstruct, a relation in other words, of weakened shadows to faded light. Each quarter we'd reserve against that, but it was never enough. Rather we could only fund indistinct mutterings, like rain drops someone might be willing to put up with, or from crisp instinct, avoid. If there were other problems that's because of things scooped out of the earth and placed on a table, forcing us to analyze them. Whereas years ago we stored memories away as reliable touchstones, and the places where they lived, graced with gems of purple microdot, would radiate out from them, with a soft, steady pulse, to signal transition to a new phase, a butterfly, in quotes, whose low monologue would draw the washed-out sky into a more convenient way to express itself, at some slack hour, when the bees slept inside their bee-forms, and the opposite of urgency wandered off unchained, nowadays we wake up and get on with whatever we have to do, most likely retrieving paperwork about the grid that's been established, in whose various quadrants phrases are plotted to represent different kinds of achievements, in particular those which caused earlier structures to lose their grip, having voiced personal feelings in a way that altered them. The house of imagination coughs. Why mention it? Clouds get ready to go, to float here but not there, opaque but clear, thick but substanceless, invoking an experience never to be had but always to be undergoing, no paradox save in resolving what never was by what never will be, openly fixed on the unfixed, cool and high, or (at that moment) low and dark under porticoes, maintained as an image or concept to be drawn through to another place where something else will have been replied to handsomely the moment its outlines become obscured, leaning back against the glass behind which a belief is packing itself up for use in rituals, holding an axe-like implement within the range of reasonable outcomes spread out below the paper hats of these wicked hills. Despite lapses, or rather because of them—extending across lines and planes into day and night the possibility that something could be massed outside the screen, altering its form by refusing to take shape, which it hadn't really looked to do, but yielded to the sweet incomparable pressure held at bay until the sky cleared and the air grew warm, only then to adopt a look of studied ruefulness, moving shyly into view but out of range, the product of thinking through all the implications with various levels of effectiveness, circling the main point—it starts to wobble. Noise drops off, driven up to treetops on a fiddle. And so we go and so we follow ourselves down into the habit of stuffing ourselves with nearby organisms, each of us seeking the endpoint of sallow foreknowledge in dismembered reasoning. Sounds good. Then let's move ahead five years to watch the light foam offsite in dreams. How to make this point on a phone call with strangers is a real issue. Is it correct to say there's too much work to be done in advance to justify taking the step of doing it, and that there's no reward significant or lasting enough to have caused us to engage this hazy destiny passing before us like a pair of unfocused eyes, blind to what holds still while everything else shuttles back and forth, mornings and evenings, wheeling over an anxious track, answering ever more specific requests with ever more detailed responses, yet even so the next day the whole thing slips by without a whisper? Do we start again, with backdated assurances that all that nonsense was legitimate nonsense—that the sounds sucked through our ears were heard exactly as they presented themselves to be heard? Time to reach back for the one word nesting there, beside the picture of the sunrise, where the tiny foreground figures gaze out with indefinite longing, or with a desire to withdraw from the scene, to take on the viewer's perspective, who has coincidentally decided to take on theirs, in some future state, when the leaves stop falling in the monotonous chill. The impulses to be unleashed then will level off in the magnetosphere, having soared over a lightless thoughtscape of wounded notes drifting out from platonic silence. Remember, remember not. Teach, lift up, enlarge, look upon, in whatever order. The day was fully nothing more than what it was. The months had crystallized into hard if forgotten facts, susceptible to local interpretation, but finally signifying one consistent intention—to benefit x by withholding from y. Raised some twelve feet above the stone floor, whose stark firmness offset any delight in elevation, we began to study the materials provided, knowing that a skunk had probed the same space scarcely an hour ago. Whose private meditations were these? Whence the fragrance permeating their desire not to be understood? A big box of facts had been sent to the wrong warehouse and retrieving it meant knifing through choked streets until hints of its presence became too vivid to ignore. At the same time events arrived from elsewhere distinguished by their implausibility. For every one hundred and eight years the locusts return to the witchwood. They offer themselves to intuition as being naively there, standing both apart and within, seeking confirmation that they are registered in some way, that the labyrinth to which they will return is for now, just now, placed in brackets, while the sun paints their walls, and lures them back toward certainty until eyes bend down to watch a monk wipe dust from a bowl. Yet you can't just look at a bowl and say, "That's a bowl." Feelings, desires, volitions get us confused. And so afternoons are spent stacking wood and stepping back to look at the contours, the lines, the gaps, the organs. Still, the tremulous thing somehow manages to stand up on its own, and tossing its splendid head, open its eyes for the first time.

The day pauses.

There are a few fundamental problems to guard against, and they actually exist, I met them. I watched them throw themselves along the edge of the road, where breezes lifted them up through the shadow of an immense ship clattering down the sky. I think it was the third of November. On that day the Venerable Ascetic, indifferent to all, shone in splendor like a golden planet or a flame without the properties of flame. A single eye beheld this more or less by accident, at the boundary of two identical landscapes, reached by ladders, one on either side of a common wall. The eye was emptied of its own nature, and left the earth in search of a medium where colors could be seen in primal clarity, subject to pure laws, and ready to shower down life and expression on whatever called up to them, not to be resolved, or fed into some exquisite mechanism, but left in abeyance, to evoke another visibility, moving abroad beforehand, in a loose and fluid framework, whose teasing limbs would give us something to feel or be felt by, lying face to face, like painted shapes, not resisting modification, not suspending pursuit.

William Fuller grew up in Barrington, Illinois, and received his PhD from the University of Virginia in 1983. His most recent books of poetry include *Hallucination* (2011), *Quorum* (2012), and *Playtime* (2015). He is Principal Advisor to the trust department at The Northern Trust Company in Chicago.